Appearance and Reality

By Bob Mumford

LIFECHANGERS ®

P.O. Box 3709 ❖ Cookeville, TN 38502
931.520.3730 ❖ lc@lifechangers.org

The Scripture quotations contained in this book are from:
   The New American Standard Bible®, Copyright ©
1960, 1962, 1963, 1971, 1972, 1973, 1975, 1977, 1995 by The
Lockman Foundation. The Amplified Bible. 1987. La Habra,
CA: The Lockman Foundation.

PLUMBLINE

Published by:

LIFECHANGERS ®
LIBRARY SERIES

P.O. Box 3709 | Cookeville, TN 38502
(800) 521-5676 | www.lifechangers.org

All Rights Reserved
ISBN 978-1-940054-14-8

© 2016 Lifechangers
All Rights Reserved
Printed in the United States of America

Appearance and Reality

By Bob Mumford

"Don't you have some really close friends?" Asked the court appointed counselor to the beaten down, disheveled little old man. "Oh, yes," he responded with some alacrity. "I have known them for years and our friendship has become quite close." "What are their names, if I may ask?" Continued the counselor. "Jim, Jack and Jose" came the immediate reply. "Their last names?" The counselor asked. "Oh, yes. Jim Beam, Jack Daniels, and Jose Cuervo," he responded without hesitation.

Many years of dealing with human beings has allowed me to understand the fact that we quite easily lose contact with Reality, escaping into various forms of denial. What is more frightening is the fact that we are unable to realize this has occurred. We are unaware that we have lost or departed from reality. As one pundit said: "I have lost reality and I do not miss it at all!"

Listen to what scripture tells us about the difference between what appears to be a solution (unreality) and the Reality of life as it actually unfolds.

Don't live carelessly, unthinkingly. Make sure you understand what the Master wants. Don't drink too much wine. That cheapens your life. Drink the Spirit of God, huge draughts of

Him. Sing hymns instead of drinking songs! Sing songs from your heart to Christ. Sing praises over everything, any excuse for a song to God the Father in the name of our Master, Jesus Christ. (Eph. 5:17-20, The Message).

The present upheavals in American politics and financial mismanagement is about to bring us all into a fresh encounter with reality. My desire is to introduce you to the philosophy of Reality, what it is and how it works. Why we are now being called upon to be awakened to this reality? What action is required to respond, properly, and responsibly?

As we proceed to unpack this idea, we will all find ourselves included and awakened in ways that we could never have imagined. The reason? Well, most of us have lost reality and do not seem to miss it at all! Listen to Jesus and His sense of Reality: "If it were not so, I would have told you…"

Introducing Philosophy of Reality

1. We live in time. Reality transcends time.

2. Time is defined as cognitive: all that we know, think, and understand as a human being. Cognitive processes have to do with the act or process of knowing and perceiving.

3. Reality is defined as meta-(signifying more than) cognitive, entering the realm of the infinite God. More than human thinking!

4. The terms are finite and infinite. Finite means all that can be seen on the earth. Infinite is more than all that is on the earth, more than all of the creation and matter itself that is unseen.

5. We have embraced life in time, in its social context. Reality does not have a beginning or an ending. Reality is more than time.

6. Reality is God and His Kingdom—all of which originated outside of time. All that the Kingdom implies, suggests, and seeks to accomplish are infinity seeking expression and purpose.

7. The mystery of the incarnation is Reality choosing to become finite, so He could reveal His infinite self to us. Jesus said, "If you have seen me, you have seen the Father" (John 14:7).

8. The church was born in time. The Kingdom of God was never born in time. Kingdom is infinite. We are born into the eternal and choose the higher order of the Kingdom of God (2 Peter 1:11).

9. Christ is the head of the church. He is, however, the embodiment of the Kingdom.

10. Church has been given reality in incarnational form and is destined for eternity.

11. Kingdom governs all concepts of church because it has no origin. The Kingdom of God is eternal, uncreated and incorruptible.

12. Kingdom is God's Reality made incarnate so that

we could participate. "What is man that You take thought of him? And the son of man that You care for him?" (Psalm 8:4).

13. If we live only in time, we have missed the issue of life that requires us to understand and embrace the new birth, become impregnated with Agape, and be introduced to God the Father Who is Reality.

14. The eternal, uncreated, incorruptible Christ is infinite. He comes for the purpose of introducing us to Reality.

15. Reality is spirit or metaphysical. The word "meta" signifies more than, moving into a dimension more than all that is physical. Those who worship in Reality are asked to "worship in spirit and in truth"(John 4:23-24). We are required to be taken out of our sphere that is cognitive and transferred into an alternate sphere that is metacognitive. The term **metacognitive** signifies possessing a higher-order of thinking skills that increase control over of our own thought processes and a capacity for deeper understanding when learning. Like "meta" explained above, we have entered a "kind of knowing" that is "spiritual" or more than human thinking. This is illustrated by the animal world. Who can discern the storm is coming, when the human seems incapacitated or ignorant? The animals are able to prepare and we do not.

16. When we speak of God as Reality, we use a capital "R". He is more than, greater than anything we have ever encountered. The fact is we need to become

adjusted to and more comfortable with entering Reality. This can be accomplished by losing our illicit fear of God (Gen. 3:10) and entering into a Kingdom value system.

17. Finite signifies all that has a beginning or an origin. If it starts, it can also stop.

18. Infinite signifies that which does not have and never has had a beginning. If it does not have a beginning, it does not have an ending. Such is the Life that Father has provided by incarnation.

19. Jesus seeks to take us to the Father; He is infinite Reality. He is, He was, and He will be! "before the foundation of the world…" (Matt. 25:34).

20. The Father, Son, and Holy Spirit do not have a beginning. Consequently, they do not have an ending. Such is eternal Life.

21. If we do not understand Reality, who He is and why He has designed and accomplished the redemptive act, we have failed to know and understand God (*Christian Appearance or Reality*, John McKay, Knox Press).

Application of our 21 point sequence: Reality asks that we seriously understand the necessity of entering fellowship with eternal Reality by the entrance that He has provided in Matthew 28: 19: "And Jesus came up and spoke to them, saying, 'All authority has been given to Me in heaven and on earth. Go therefore and make disciples of all the nations, *baptizing them in the name of the Father and the Son and the Holy Spirit*, teaching them to observe all that I commanded you; and lo, I am with you always, even to the end of the age.'"

Several lessons in Reality:

a. Reality and infinity have come to earth by incarnation, God made man.
b. Reality asks us to respond to His incarnational act through Love.
c. Mentor and baptize them *into* Reality, the Trinity (Father, Son and Holy Spirit) (Matt.28:19).
d. God, in Himself as Trinity, is a "sweet society."
e. Intention is how to know and participate with Reality.
f. Reality: knowing God in Trinitarian fullness (John 17:3).
g. Reality brings a new, unknown value system to be observed.
h. Being baptized is to be introduced into God's sweet society in the Trinity.
i. Jesus says, "Because I am Reality and Truth, I, Myself, will be with you always, even to the end" (Matt 28:20).

Behavioral Change as Evidence of Reality

We have attempted a free association understanding of what it means to be introduced to Reality. What we need to do now is embrace this value system that has just been introduced. Listen again to the instructions from Jesus in Matt. 28:20: "Teach them to observe all that I commanded you!" Father's value system is that which He seeks to give to the world by means of His Own incarnational people. He is our Gift.

However, we are His gift to those whom He loves and seeks. The necessity of being incarnational, implies God, in His eternal purpose, has chosen to give Himself to us by means of incarnating Himself into the person of Jesus Christ—God With Us.

My personal conviction is that the manner of presentation and application of Christ and His redemptive act has served to enervate (weaken and debilitate), if not castrate the necessity of the change in human behavior. All that belongs to the Kingdom is behavioral. We have been introduced to God's Own Sphere, and He is requiring us to learn to behave. We have taken His Name and His governmental reality upon ourselves.

In this section, I hope to introduce you to the idea and the pure joy of learning to "please God the Father." Become a Father-pleaser, as a deliberate gift to Him, for His drawing us to Himself by means of the Person of Christ (John 6:44 and 65). If you are willing, try to see Reality seeking you in these two instructional insights from John:

No one can come to Me [Jesus] unless the Father who sent Me draws him; and I will raise him up on the last day (John 6:44).

And He [Jesus] was saying, "For this reason I have said to you, that no one can come to Me unless it has been granted him from the Father" (John 6:65).

Our understanding, from these scriptures is not complicated. He has drawn us to Himself for the purpose of instructing us in His own value system. Ones, of whom He identifies, as "'the Lord knows those that are His...'" (2 Tim. 2:19). Such is family, relational, and purposeful. Having a Kingdom value system means being filled with reality and destiny.

We are now seeking to move our thinking and our emotions toward understanding and embracing Father's own value system. It is something Jesus introduced to us as our obeying the great commission: "*teach them to observe all that I commanded you*" (Matt 28:20). To state it simply, this is what Father has requested. This is what will please Him. Learning to please God as a Father never touches upon religious works. We are learning Agape responses. We can make this clear and applicable.

Reality is metaphysical. We have embraced and been inseminated with something in the realm of the Spirit that has changed the manner in which we think, talk, walk, and respond. That Reality is identified as a Being, a Person, more than a Person. He is wholly infinite, wholly transcendent. Father chose to become incarnate in the person of Christ in order for us to enter the route or the Way He has provided so that we could come to know Him, learn who He is, and how to please Him. Learning to please Him will keep us in Reality!

The impact of what it means to please God as my Father is what has changed my own behavior. When I presented this idea at a large conference, one well-known and influential speaker said to me: "In all my years, I have never heard anything like this. It has moved me, deeply." Consider the following scriptures as we focus on the reality of becoming a Father-pleaser like Christ Jesus.

1. Jesus said, "And He who sent Me is with Me; He has not left Me alone, for I always do the things that are *pleasing* to Him" (John 8:29).
2. "Therefore we also have as our ambition, whether at home or absent, to be *pleasing* to Him" (2 Cor. 5:9).
3. "Trying to learn what is *pleasing* to the Lord" (Eph. 5:10).
4. "But just as we have been approved by God to be entrusted with the gospel, so we speak, not as *pleasing* men, but God who examines our hearts" (1 Thess. 2:4).
5. "They are not *pleasing* to God, but hostile to all men (1 Thess. 2:15).
6. "By faith Enoch was taken up so that he would not see death; and He was not found because God took Him up; for he obtained the witness that before his being taken up he was *pleasing* to God" (Heb. 11:5).

7. "Now the God of peace, who brought up from the dead the great Shepherd of the sheep through the blood of the eternal covenant, even Jesus our Lord, equip you in every good thing to do His will, working in us that which is *pleasing* in His sight, through Jesus Christ, to whom be the glory forever and ever. Amen" (Heb. 13:20-21).
8. "And whatever we ask we receive from Him, because we keep His commandments and do the things that are *pleasing* in His sight" (1 John 3:22). Notice how John sees this idea of pleasing Father. Compare the first and the last verses; prayers are answered out of a personal relationship with Him and because we are *pleasing*! It is not "works" but a promised response from a Father.

The hidden mysteries of the Kingdom of God can be discovered by those seeking Reality. It depends upon our personal encounter of our human self with Father, who is Reality—Agape that presents Himself as an absolute truth. All spiritual growth or maturity (Greek: telios) depends upon and proceeds from the encounter. Failure or refusal to encounter that Reality precipitates conscious or unconscious, departure from Reality: I have lost touch with Reality and do not miss it (Him) at all! Is it possible for me to have never recognized this realm and never know His drawing me?

God said to the children of Israel when they disobeyed Him, "I brought you into the fruitful land, to eat its fruit and its good things. But you came and defiled My land, And My inheritance you made an abomination. The priests did not say, 'Where is the Lord?' And those who handle the law did not know Me; The rulers also transgressed against Me, and the prophets prophesied by Baal and walked after things that did not profit" (Jer. 2:7-8).

Much of institutional Christianity has retreated to symbol, assumption, tradition, and doctrinal certainty. All of which creates more shadow in appearance, in contrast with Reality. We have been capacitated to know and enjoy a new and different insight into the dimension of the realm in which God dwells, the Spirit realm by means of the new birth. In that encounter, God inseminates us with the "Spirit of Christ," allowing and enabling us to know, hear, feel, and understand the communication system of God and His governmental Kingdom.

By entering a clear, biblical understanding of a Kingdom, a Father, and a value system, Reality has a way of making His Presence known. Abiding in the Reality of becoming Father-pleaser results in life-giving fruit appearing on the vine. We, again, begin to move toward a maturity for which the hurting world has been waiting.

Kingdom has been avoided, sublimated, dismissed, and ignored for the primary reason that it requires/demands spiritual Reality in order for it to function and present itself. To fight or resist the unshakable Kingdom Reality is to fight and resist Life itself. For example R.A. Torrey like other authors does not even have a category entitled Kingdom within the pages of his book on Biblical Themes entitled: *The New Topical Textbook*. Protestant creeds, we have discovered, are church-centered, failing to present and explain the priority of Kingdom of God. The ignorance and neglect of the Kingdom as the central theme of scripture is nothing less than spectacular.

Religious culture, tradition, and custom all move us toward nominalism and illiteracy toward spiritual things. The end result is passivity—eager to remain undisturbed. As we lose the centrality of the Kingdom as its biblical theme, we lose all governmental strength. Appearance by itself is nothing less than hypocrisy to those observing from the hurting world. Jesus says, "Why do you call Me Lord, Lord," when all of these other things rule your behavior? (Luke 6:46).

The essence of Reality is measurable by behavioral change. That change is due, directly, to our learning to please God as a Father. God is Agape. The "fruit of the Spirit" (Matt. 7:16) is the manifestation of Agape that has been:

A. Incarnated in human form through the new birth (John 3:1).
B. The insemination has been accomplished by means of an eternal, uncreated, and incorruptible Seed (1 Peter 1:23).
C. The fact that it is a Seed implies human responsibility to become engaged and activated. We are required to cultivate, nourish, and bring

that seed to its biblical maturity: 30/60/100 fold (Mark 4:8).

D. The Seed, cultivated in a Kingdom, governmental context brings forth those whose desire is to learn to please God as a Father. The idea of being under His government, with Jesus as our King, speaks of a new and different value system and one that we have embraced as our own. This is who we are!

E. Observable behavioral change becomes the living proof that we have, authentically, engaged and submitted to Kingdom reality. This is called epistemological, the theme of John's first epistle.

F. Kingdom is recognizable by reason that my behavior is now replicating Jesus Christ as a Father-pleaser. His Agape, birthed in me, is changing and re-aligning my own DNA. I am being "conformed into the Image of Jesus Christ" (Rom.8:29).

G. Others, observing this Kingdom transformation, give testimony that Reality, and not appearance, has been working in our human personality.

H. Kingdom involves cognitive behavioral therapy, which I will address next. What we must not miss is the identified, Kingdom sequence that Paul provides for us.

For the kingdom of God is not eating and drinking, but righteousness and peace and joy in the Holy Spirit. For he who in this way serves Christ is acceptable to God and approved by men (Rom 14:17-18).

a. *Righteousness*: This is "right behavior" not Christ's gift.
b. *Peace*: This is governmental. Only within good government can there be peace ruled by the Prince of Peace—internal and external.
c. *Joy*: Such is not fun, happiness, personal fulfillment but Joy as the mark of Agape maturity — full acceptance of Father's value system.

Apart from a governmental type of Kingdom, with its incarnated value system presented by Christ and its requirement for Reality, the absolute nature and purpose of Agape becomes suspect. All "religion" becomes "the opiate of the people". "Religion is the opium of the people" is a quote attributed to Karl Marx. He could see that religious appearance lacked the Realty for which it stood. Accusations against overly religious individuals and groups abound and much of that opposition, we may have actually earned!

It is the dramatic and measurable "fruit" of Agape that alters human behavior and testifies of our having surrendered our own personal sovereignty to the person of Christ enabling the Lord to make the necessary changes within our own personality. Failure to change does not endanger my salvation. It does, however, damage my journey into Reality and the joy of coming to know God. Agape, when seen and embraced as an absolute, insists that my behavior and my governing value system give evidence that my desire is to do you good.

How God anointed and consecrated Jesus of Nazareth with the [Holy] Spirit and with strength and ability and power; **how He went about doing good** *and, in particular, curing all who were harassed and oppressed by [the power of] the devil, for God was with Him* (Acts 10:38).

So then, as occasion and opportunity open up to us, **let us do good** *[morally]* **to all people** *[not only being useful or profitable to them, but also doing what is for their spiritual good and advantage]. Be mindful to be a blessing, especially to those of the household of faith [those who belong to God's family with you, the believers]* (Gal 6:10).

We must acknowledge that Christ and His People doing good is the value added. Good is that which Father has been eager to give to the world. When He gives, people respond. When we give, people respond.

My desire and behavior does not arise from within my own person/personality but from the origin of the new birth and the Kingdom transformation. I am experiencing Reality from my encounters as He has come to us in the Person of Christ, Agape made Incarnate. God, as a Father has imparted His value system to us in the form of the eternal, uncreated, and incorruptible Seed. This value system, under the title of "Kingdom," carries with it creative action. Such creativity is much more than correct adherence to accepted doctrine.

Presentation of a Non-Religious Value System

There has been given to us an insight into the word: *Basilea,* which is the Greek word used by Jesus for the Kingdom. The word contains fresh thinking that demonstrates the ability to bring hope and workable answers at a time when we personally thought there might not be any answers. Through personal encounter with this Basilea, I can introduce you to concepts of an invisible governing reality, which functions in realms both good and bad. Basilea is a concept of reality, applicable to all, containing the very content of an urgently needed understanding of the invisible, governmental sphere. Simply stated, we really do need more than that which meets the eye! Hence: metaphysical and metacognitive.

1. The most basic of all ingredients of Kingdom (Basilea) philosophy has been reduced to two very foundational and imperative qualifications. These are the keys to the Kingdom:

> A. Do what you promise.
> B. Do not encroach upon that which is another's (Richard Maybury).

2. The most workable insight into the Kingdom (Basilea) philosophy can be summarized in three statements:

A. I am now personally seeking to do you good.

B. The desire to do you good is not my own. My desire arises out of my value system, which originates in the Kingdom of God.

C. Presently, I am now anticipating an occasion to do you good!

3. The most necessary aspect of Kingdom philosophy is the simple, straightforward statement that says: If I am unable or restrained from doing you good, I promise never intentionally to do you harm. I keep my promises.

4. The most important feature of the Kingdom philosophy is the necessity of our engaging an awakening of the five subjective senses: see, hear, feel, taste, and smell, in the realm of the metacognitive. It is these five senses that provide both the motive and the capacity for us to transition into that Kingdom or governmental sphere. It is entrance to the metacognitive, which produces the metanarrative, which is the content or quintessence of our story. The metaphysical and metacognitive have become the basis of all physics and science within our recent cosmic understanding. The Kingdom of God is within.

5. The most crucial phase of the human dimension of the Kingdom philosophy is for us to recover our ability to tell our story and sing our song in an authentic manner and with worthy motive. Failure or refusal to do so may cause us to go to our grave with our story untold and our song unsung! Preservation of personal

Reality is more critical than we have understood.

We all know that the poet can express in a few words what is needing to be communicated. Such is this prose, which has served me for many years keeping me in Reality:

The Man Who Knew:

The Dreamer visioned Life as it might be,
And from his dream forthright a picture grew;
A painting all the people thronged to see,
And joyed therein — till came *the Man Who Knew*,
Saying: "Tis bad! Why do you gape you fools!
He paints not according to the schools."

The Dreamer probed Life's mystery of woe,
And in a book he sought to give the clue;
The people read, and saw that it was so,
And read again — then came *the Man Who Knew*,
Saying: "You witless ones! This book is vile:
It does not have the rudiments of style."

Love smote the Dreamer's lips, and silver clear
He sang a song so sweet, so tender true,
Till all the market-place was thrilled to hear,
And listened rapt — till came *the Man Who Knew*,
Saying: "His technique is wrong; he sings ill,
Waste not your time." The singer's voice was still.
And then the people roused as if from sleep,
Crying: "What care we if it be not Art!"

Has he not charmed us, made us laugh and weep?
Come, let us crown him where he sits apart."
Then, with his picture spurned, his book unread,
His song unsung, they found their Dreamer — *dead*.

Robert Service, Rhymes of a Rolling Stone.

Five Ways to Identify our own Response to Reality

Embrace

PROBLEM

Self-deception and faulty patterns of thinking are most complicated. We worry about others "leading us astray." That is a possibility. What is more prevalent and much more difficult to engage is when we, due to these four "escape mechanisms" manage to deceive ourselves so completely. This bit of prose that I memorized from an unknown author has helped me over the years. It may help you see how manner self-deception and the irrational thoughts of humankind actually work:

> I do not love you, Dr. Fell.
> The reasons *why*, I cannot tell.
> But this I know and know quite well;
> I do not love you, Dr. Fell!

When facing a problem and the Word of the Lord comes to us, seeking to awaken and reveal Himself to us, there are the five possible responses. Our picture is Reality has now coming knocking on our door. Every difficult situation or Life Lab has been designed to break my illusion and open me to my Father and my Father to me (1 Cor. 8:3).

Our first and almost autonomic reaction is to deny. Denial is not a river in Egypt called "De-Nile." Denial is the first-fruit of our tendency to want to "run, hide or shift blame." It is alive and well in the larger body of Christ. All of us have experienced going into denial. Denial is best illustrated by Abraham and Sarah's famous laugh when they heard the word of the angel telling her she would have a child (Gen. 17:17 & 18:12). It is a pure form of denial. Sarah said in her heart, "this cannot be," and she gave all of her cognitive reasons based on human knowledge. Her mind rebeled and her emotions followed. She knew God could do many things, but this promise was too much. Personally, I too, have experienced clear denial on several occasions, only to hear the Lord remind me, "More than you can ask or think" (Eph. 3:20).

The second possible response is to avoid. We very carefully work our way around the problem in order to continue on our own way, undisturbed! We are unwilling, simply do not want to face it, or fear we are inadequate to deal with the problem. Avoidance is another form of denial but much more subtle. It is playing intellectual and emotional games with ourselves for the purpose of getting our own way. We seek to avoid people, issues, problems, and certain conversations. Circumvention, knowing how to "get around it" becomes an acquired skill like abiding. Avoiding begins a journey into unreality, disillusionment, and living in appearance rather than Reality.

The third one is to endure. We enter the circumstance but do so with deep, internal resistance.

This is how we actually survive the time factor, yet remain unaffected or unchanged. We are describing how a person can survive four years in the military or ten years in prison and learn nothing. He/she simply endures in prison. All they are concerned about is "doing the time." Many of us have learned to endure our marriage in a similar manner. We do not yield or seek to discover how we could change; we just endure the thing. In Christian experience, we can endure Sunday morning. We can endure Father's request or commission with an attitude of waiting until this is over. Carefully examined, we are insisting on "having my own way." We have missed the Reality that our Lord has been offering His unbelievable offer of His friendship (John 15:15).

The fourth one is more drastic—to turn back. This is what Israel attempted coming out of Egypt for they missed the "leeks and the onions" (Num. 11:5). Listen as the writer to the Hebrews explains the idea of turning back. "And truly, if they had been mindful of that country from whence they came out, they might have had opportunity to have returned" (Heb. 11:15).

As most of you know, immediately after my encounter with reality when I was first saved at age 12, I turned back as a new believer. I did not want to go on into this new and unexplored world of the Kingdom of God. Few things give us a clearer insight into the twisted nature of fallen man than a clear insight into how easily we can turn back after all the demonstration of God's love in the Person of Christ.

Paul asks the Galatian believers:

> *But now that you have come to know God, or rather to be known by God, how is it that you turn back again to the weak and worthless elemental things, to which you desire to be enslaved all over again?* (Gal 4:9).

The fifth, and biblical response, is to embrace. Walking into Reality, holding our heavenly Father's hand is the chosen alternative to all four responses. Many of life's "happenings" present themselves to us as sophisticated occasions to run, hide, shift blame. The only way out is abiding in Reality. This is God's prescription in John 15:7-10:

> *If you abide in Me, and My words abide in you, ask whatever you wish, and it shall be done for you. By this is My Father glorified, that you bear much fruit, and so prove to be My disciples. Just as the Father has loved (Agape) Me, I have also loved (Agape) you; abide in My love (Agape).*

You must see that Abiding requires confidence in Father's nature. Knowing Him is the only manner in which we can embrace situations. We are in the middle of a problem in circumstances that we would prefer to avoid, when everything within us wants to deny what is happening. It has been most demanding to say and believe that God in these circumstances intends to do me good! My whole being is crying out to grit my teeth and endure. Pressures are multiplying that say, "You had better turn back, or you will perish out here in this wilderness." It is then we are able to say, "Father, I am yours. You know I do believe that You are able to work all things together for good because I love You. My focus is on You. You are the object of my affection." It is only our love (Agape) for God, Who enables our proper response to His love.

He "uses all things" for the purpose of presenting circumstances that serve the purposes of God in our life. In my response, I am embracing the issues, however unpleasant or demanding. Holding to the value system to which I have committed has been designed to bring me to behavioral transformation and increased intimacy with God, who is pure Reality. He is not worried about His Own Reality. His purpose is to rescue us out of our illusion, the one we so reluctantly surrender. When we do surrender, the freedom, the joy, and the light of life flows over our entire being. We grow by getting all of the juice out of the orange, before we discard the skin.

Philosophy of the Kingdom Reality that Transforms our Behavior by Means of Cognitive Behavior Therapy

The Absolute Reality does not begin by asking us to love (Agape) others. This has proven to be essentially impossible. We need to be equipped, mentored, and given proper examples. He begins by asking us to Love (Agape) Him: heart, soul, mind, and strength. Our love for Him serves as our priority. Our love for Him gives us insight and motivation. My love for Him moves me, behaviorally, to love (Agape) who and what He loves. "God so loved the [hurting] world that He gave" (John 3:16). Oh, the sheer joy of coming to love the lost! He was a "friend to sinners"!

Cognitive behavioral therapy states that our patterns of thinking, choices of behaviors, and emotions are profoundly interrelated. My intention in presenting the cognitive behavioral therapy is for the purpose of introducing what could prove to be an innovative behavioral theory that may be identified as "metacognitive behavioral therapy" proposed by the Father applying Agape as an absolute when He decided to reveal Himself in incarnational form. Note the far-reaching implications of Acts 17:31, "Because He has fixed a day in which He will judge the world in righteousness through a Man whom He has appointed, having furnished proof to all men by raising Him from the dead."

God the Father, I am persuaded, could see that my actions of being and becoming a confirmed and mature "taker" could be transformed, behaviorally, into that of being and becoming a mature "giver." Such cognitive or metacognitive movement would transform my thoughts, as well as serve to govern and adjust my feelings. Out of such metacognitive therapy, I could know freedom and engage experientially in an authentic personal behavior transformation. Hope then says, "Yes, Father has made a way for me to become more like Jesus!"

Kingdom as contrasted to religion, used in its negative form, introduces engaging the Absolute in the embrace of His governmental Kingdom, which functions in mystery, paradox, and contradiction, i.e., God is Agape and He loves the World [cosmos or all creation that groans and suffers]! This Reality also fills the role of being our Creator and Father. He intends that we be enabled to encounter a deep, mystical, and metaphysical desire to imitate and effectively participate in His Agape for this hurting world system. This "sound" or call has been identified in John 6:44 and 65. This factor, alone, transcends the superficiality of present day Christendom. The "kosmos" in the Greek of John 3:16, speaking of that which Father has placed His Agape must be understood as "His Command"—an expression of Who He is and What He wants. Our immediate response must be analogous to that of Christ. He loved what/who Father loved. The value system suggests that we too are to be mentored to love that hurting world in a manner demonstrated in the life and ministry of our Lord Jesus.

Awakened, from our cognitive world of being and becoming an increasingly mature taker, we are surprised to discover that we do have and may have always had an innate, metaphysical desire (Greek: epithumia) to participate in Father's Agape for the hurting world. Religion has:

1. Injured, corrupted, or prostituted that desire
2. Dulled or numbed our sensory receptors
3. Confused the essential issues
4. Disallowed our participation with conscience and freedom
5. Consequently, the new birth is necessary to re-engage us into His Person

Conflict continues to rage in our mind and within our human spirit. Suddenly, due to that awakening, we may discover ourselves eager to be and become a person who "gives" and refuses to continue to "take" in an illegal, self-serving manner. We desire, amazingly enough, to become involved. For us to see the Kingdom in biblical terms signifies that we may now, envision, see ourselves becoming free from being a taker. Authentic hope engages—a hope that does not "make me ashamed."

The paradox and the contradictions, which surround the consummate decision whether to be and become a giver or to continue to be and become a taker, no longer hold that strong, paralyzing sway in my thinking or in my feelings. We are beginning to experience and think freedom. Free from being a taker. Transformed and saturated with deep, personal desire to be and become a giver. This is the source of Joy!

If you can see Christ as a giver, you may also

see the Father! The standard of being a giver in the Kingdom is the Father, Himself (Mt 5:48). Christ, it is recorded, never "sinned" (Heb. 4:15). He never, on any occasion, became a taker. He effectively, demonstrated Agape as a giver revealing God's glory. Never "coming short of that glory."

When you see us, who seek to embrace the reality of that Kingdom, you may also be enabled to spiritually see our Father by means of our family value system. We are givers and not takers because we seek to reveal God, as a true Father, to those who have been blinded, injured, and offended. This Father has already proven His love for us in the gift of His Son. Hopefully, due to a fresh emphasis on Agape, we may yet also see Father more perfectly revealed in the body of Christ (Eph. 6:24 NASB).

The idea of the "user" is included under the heading of the taker. A user is one who functions, almost exclusively, in a utilitarian manner, using people for his own agenda or personal advantage. The term may help us expand the idea and application for the urgency and importance of our theme. It is the taker/user who, most often, introduces the theme of corruption into each and every aspect of life and society. This is not superficial or irrelevant. The more I am able to think this through, the more I am convinced we have engaged one of the most serious theme in all of Scripture. Perhaps, it may prove to be the theme for which Jesus died! It would appear so from a casual reading of Romans 8:19-21:

For the creation waits with eager longing for the revealing of the sons of God. For the creation was subjected to futility not willingly, but because of him who subjected it, in hope that the creation itself will be set free from its bondage to corruption and obtain the freedom of the glory of the children of God.

We may have sort of stumbled upon this diagnostic insight, which when closely examined, begins to yield answers as to the manner and method that humankind and society in general can be transformed. In some critical manner, we are now waiting for some answer that seems to elude us. Try examining, considering the following:

a. Wall Street taker: like Madoff; oppressive banking system. The rigged stock market. The con games. Seduction. Increasingly, stock market known for being rigged.

b. Government taker, in greed and pride causing 14,000 wars. This number being only the ones known in history.

c. Sexual taker: predators of sexual rape, child porno, etc. User may enable us to understand the sexual taker more perfectly.

d. Religious taker: religion, as a system, has become a sophisticated taker. John Oman says, "Except for Divine Intervention, religion would be the most corrupt institution in the world." How many times does Scripture speak of the widows and widow's houses, the orphan and disadvantaged needing to be protected and guarded from taker/users? (James 1:26-27)

e. Social taker: the social "engineer" who know how to manipulate the laws, rules, and the peoples themselves to their own profit. Every project paid under the table; over budgeted; skimmed.

f. Family taker: a mother/father who becomes a user of their own children. Abusive, manipulative, incestuous. India allowed me to talk to a child whose hands had been amputated so that they could beg for the family on the street more profitably.

g. Medical taker: drug companies, surgical procedures, and practices that are designed to enrich and promote the doctor's role as the giver, while functioning as a taker!

h. Psychological/Counselor takers: known abuse and cultivated dependence within this discipline. The fees continue while the answers disappear.

i. Educational system: Only time will reveal the depth of corruption and failure within the school systems of our nation. The loss of Reality is so deep, pervasive, and complex as to defy solution.

Corruption, displayed in all of its sophisticated forms, seems to fall quite easily under the rubric of taker. In the realms of politics, finance, religion, natural family, social workers, education, medicine, and all other forms of functional care, we have been disillusioned with the ones charged, identified, and titled with being a "giver" only to discover that giver has been transformed into a taker. Many of these have earned the title taker in the most mature definition of that word! Religion, particularly, has been identified and labeled as a taker.

Identification and cessation of illegal taking by a fresh emphasis on the Kingdom brings forth effective and trustworthy givers, who will, without question, move us, our families, our churches, our cities, and our nations toward the freedom that Christ has promised in John 8:29-32: "and you will know the truth, and the truth will make you free." When I began to open this theme, I had no idea of the magnitude and pervasiveness that was about to be uncovered. We may be able to solidify this concept of giving/taking by observing something that I have previously been unable to see: All biblical "works of the flesh," to my surprise, fall into the category of being some form of taking.

Reality in Proposition

Take time to Listen: Hillsong UNITED Oceans (Where Feet May Fail) Lyric Video https://youtu.be/dy9nwe9_xzw

My first attempt was to present something of a "route" or some kind of attitude or posture that would enable us to be and become Father-pleasers. These points and the following prayer to God are quite personal.

"God, my Father: My deepest desire is not only to follow Jesus and seek to obey Him, but to learn to please You, as a father, in a manner demonstrated and taught by Christ. I too, would like You to say to me: "Well done. You are a son/daughter in whom I am well pleased" (Matt. 3:17). This desire, now expressed, I understand, will serve to keep me in spiritual Reality, by reason of my intention to learn to please You. Your example and Agape incarnated in the Person of Christ is my value system. You and Your pleasure have become my priority. My responses have been adjusted from reluctance to hear and transformed into eagerness to respond due to my awakened love for You as eternal Father!"

Picture the image of a motor that is running loud and strong but there is no movement in rear tires. Why? Something has happened to the car's transmission. Broken? Damaged? It simply may not be in gear! This metaphor illustrates how we might read the written word of God but be missing the Rhema word from the Holy Spirit. Jesus said it quite simply: "If you Love (Agape) Me, you will ...[follow Me and love]" (John 14:23-25). As strange as it sounds, Agape is the transmission that connects the engine to the wheels so it can go.

Reality suggests responding to God with a "heart response." My deepest desire is not only to obey but also assume personal responsibility to be pleasing to Him. Such a desire expressed seems to suggest something deeper than obedience, a heart response in accordance to the laws and principles of Agape and His Kingdom value system.

One day I was driving down the road and saw a homeless woman. The Lord, quite strongly, gave me a Rhema word when He showed me that I should stop and give her $20. Knowing what is best, I only gave her $5. As I backed away from her, I suddenly became aware that I had not fully embraced and obeyed the direction of the Holy Spirit. Reluctantly, I returned to her and said, "Do you believe in God?" She responded, immediately and without hesitation. I said: "God, your Father, told me to give you this." When I gave her the $20 she burst into joy. Her spontaneous response was to start kissing my hand and up my arm. I do not know what it meant to her but the Lord knew. It was a humbling experience. For both of us, it was an issue of pleasing the Father. This became more than doctrine or rules about giving. At first I had missed an opportunity to obey from my heart. When I returned to please God, Father's joy was released in both of us.

The following six paragraphs seek to grasp the lessons from this living illustration.

1. Perfunctory personal sovereignty rather than heart obedience seems to be the very first cause of our missing the mark and missed opportunity. It is

preference for Father's pleasure and relationship rather than the temporal rewards of having our own way. Such ungoverned desire, my way rather than His way, causes or precipitates a flood of caution, reexamination, and reluctance to proceed or obey due to what it may cost me personally.

2. I am increasingly persuaded that self-awareness is the nature and essence of sin, understood as missing the mark. In application, it is a priority choice. Me now and me first, rather than Father's purpose and Father's glory!

3. Every failure, even opportunity to please Him, and every "life lab" seem to have as their spiritual purpose, the intentionality of reversing our profound propensity toward being a taker. This is a 180 degree turn to God now, God first, and a Kingdom centered value system. We choose to have Kingdom priority focused on Father's pleasure and His predestined desire, "God is all in all!"

4. Self-awareness requires me to decide in some arbitrary manner what is good and what is evil. This is followed by absolute human confidence, professional opinion, and plethora of doctrinal answers. While my own opinions may not be wrong, my own reluctance always seems injuriously inadequate.

5. Self-awareness then constitutes the nature of the fall. It is incremental and progressive. My own reluctance moves inexorably toward eros becoming telios (mature) and the five "I wills of Satan":

> *But you said in your <u>heart</u>, "I will ascend to heaven; I will raise my throne above the stars of God, And I will sit on the mount of assembly In the recesses of the north. I will ascend above the heights of the clouds; I will make myself like the Most High* (Isaiah 14:13-14).

6. As preparation for us to enter His governmental value system, Father designed us to engage death and resurrection in water baptism to begin to know how to "act against myself"—how to readjust self-awareness. Reality or the force of Agape re-aligns our DNA so that we can become "one with God" in a manner analogous with that of His incarnate Son (Rom. 8:29). When we are able to describe this in prose, it looks like this:

Ritual and Reality: Darrell Scott

Baptized in water, I simply got wet.
While none of my spiritual needs had been met
I tried to be better, I acted the part
I said the right words from my mind, not my heart.
I worked and performed and I gave it my best,
But knew in my heart that I failed every test.
Frustrated and angry, I gave up — and then,
Awareness through stillness arose from within.
The peace and the joy that had long been denied,
Were there all along – simply hidden inside.
Through yielding and stillness, true strength I did find,

The treasure within me, a source so divine.
Not might, nor can power force open the door,
But stillness releases our spirits to soar.

Reality that Serves to Take us Full Circle

We are all weary of words. Weary of roaring engines that cannot move. Weary of "devotionals ad nausea" that seek to reinforce the raw reasons we have lost or departed from Reality. Spend some time and think this through. Make an effort to gain insight, spiritually, to the incremental progression of what it means to invite God, absolute Reality, into my fragile, limited person/personality:

1. God is Agape. Agape is God. He is absolute Reality.
2. Agape is Father's solitary value system.
3. The value system presented has 5 non-religious points (pgs.18-20) because it represents a governing Reality; not more religion.
4. The Kingdom of God's value system serves as ultimate "quality control." Our Agape fruit is measurable. It is, when understood, God's Gift to the World.
5. Engaging the Kingdom value system forces us to Reality, inexorably.
6. All takers are revealed by an individualistic approach to life, rather than relational unity. Taking inevitably causes relational fractures and

failures. Fission is corruption and being committed to that which is dying.

7. Following Jesus as a giver who is focused on being a Father-Pleaser is what enables me to participate in His Kingdom purpose for others.

8. Fusion, the mystery of oneness, is the fruit of Christ and His value system, embracing all that is Light and Life.

9. We need the Rhema words or Father's spoken word through the Holy Spirit that releases "Spirit and Life" (John 6:63). Rhema comes as the result of learning to please Father.

10. Hearing, embracing, and responding to Father's Rhema Word is more expensive than we have been taught. Jesus gave full disclosure. He told us it would be expensive, and we should not expect less!

11. Turbulence, cost, contradiction, and confusion that surround learning to please God may tempt us to deny, avoid, or turn back to our "three closest friends," Jim, Jack, and Jose. In midst of being shaken, we must not receive our inspiration from "the wine" of our own thought processes but from the Rhema of the Holy Spirit (Eph. 5:17-20).

12. If we are too religious to consider the first three. Consider these other three: Religious fantasy; prescription drugs, or becoming "double-minded and unstable" (James 1:8). As we sought to demonstrate, we will attempt anything to deny; avoid, endure, or turn back.

Summary

Jesus, whom we have chosen to follow, is the Son of Man. He will, as we follow, put us on a trajectory Paul identified as setting all humanity free from corruption. "For the anxious longing of the creation waits eagerly for the revealing of the sons of God. For the creation was subjected to futility, not willingly, but because of Him who subjected it, in hope that the *creation itself also will be set free from its slavery to corruption into the freedom of the glory of the children of God.* For we know that the whole creation groans and suffers the pains of childbirth together until now" (Rom 8:19-22).

It may be hard to hear, but the biblical fact is clear: creation's freedom depends upon the freedom experienced by God's Own People. The Kingdom of God as Reality is not asking, seeking, studying for the purpose of knowing. "Knowledge puffs up" (1 Cor. 8:1). Agape builds up! Our prayer is: "I am asking You, Father, will you teach me to know you in Reality and learn to please You? You continue to be God. I will continue to be and become human as you originally created. Jesus will take me to you, by realigning my DNA to function like His. I want to know you."

LIFECHANGERS ®

P.O. Box 3709 ❖ Cookeville, TN 38502
931.520.3730 ❖ lc@lifechangers.org

www.ingramcontent.com/pod-product-compliance
Lightning Source LLC
Chambersburg PA
CBHW071752020426
42331CB00008B/2288